THE NATIONAL TRUST

Investigating THE TUDORS

By Alison Honey
Illustrated by Peter Stevenson

Contents

BACKGROUND TO THE TUDORS

The Tudor period which lasted from 1485 to 1603 is one of the most exciting in English history. It was a time when the first Englishman sailed round the world, when the first European settlers sailed the thousands of miles across the Atlantic Ocean to try to start up a new life in America and when Spain tried to invade England. It also has some of the most colourful kings and queens in England's history.

The Tudor dynasty

Since the middle of the fifteenth century two of the most powerful families in England – the Houses of Lancaster and York, both descendants of King Edward III – had been fighting each other for the throne. The Yorkist symbol was a white rose, and the Lancastrians fought under the banner of a red rose, and so these years of civil war became known as the Wars of the Roses.

RICHARD III

THE WARS OF THE ROSES

Wicked Uncle Richard

Edward IV, the head of the Yorkists, ruled England from 1461 until his death in 1483; he left as his heir a young boy who was not old enough to take over the throne. Edward's youngest brother ruled the country in place, declaring himself King Richard III. Edward IV's two young sons lived in the Tower of London while Richard was on the throne.

Meanwhile the Lancastrians were trying to work out how to overthrow Richard III. The heir to the Lancastrian title was Henry Tudor who had been born in Wales but was taken abroad to safety in France as a boy.

Into battle

In 1485 Henry Tudor decided that he should make his move as Richard III was becoming more and more unpopular. Richard had imprisoned many members of noble families who were a threat to his power and there were strong rumours that he had even murdered Edward IV's two sons.

Henry landed in Wales in August 1485 and marched east to meet Richard III, picking up support on the way. The two sides met at Bosworth Field in Leicestershire on 22 August: Richard III was killed in the battle, known as the Battle of Bosworth Field, and Henry was crowned Henry VII of England – the first of the five Tudor monarchs.

A lucky escape

Richard Edgcumbe of Cotehele in Cornwall was one of the knights who fought for Henry Tudor. Two years earlier he had supported the Duke of Buckingham's plot to overthrow Richard III but the plan was defeated, Buckingham was executed and Edgcumbe had had to hide to save his life. Richard III's agent, Sir Henry Trenowth of Bodrugan, a particularly ruthless man, tracked Edgcumbe down to Cotehele but Edgcumbe escaped down a drain-pipe, cut a sentry's throat and ran away, pursued by Trenowth's men. He was a quick thinker and when he reached the river, he took off his cap, threw it into the water and then hid in the bushes. When Trenowth's men saw his hat floating in the river they assumed that Edgcumbe had drowned himself and gave up the search. Edgcumbe managed to escape to Brittany and joined forces with Henry Tudor.

Sweet revenge

Edgcumbe got his own back on Trenowth when he was made a knight by Henry VII and given his enemy's land as a reward for his loyalty at the Battle of Bosworth Field. The story goes that Edgcumbe got his revenge by chasing Trenowth over the Cornish cliffs and into the sea at a spot which is now known as Bodrugan's Leap.

COTEHELE

Signs of the times

Important Tudor families often had their own family symbol. For example, Margaret Beaufort, Henry's mother – and one of the most educated women of the day – had a portcullis as her symbol. This became part of the Tudor badge. Look out for it when you visit buildings from this period, like The Vyne and Ightham Mote.

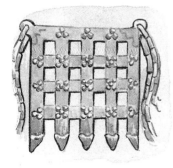

Other Tudor clues to look for:

The Tudor Rose

A double rose showing both the families of York (the white rose) and Lancaster (the red rose), united after the Wars of the Roses through Henry Tudor's marriage to Edward IV's daughter, Elizabeth of York

Places to look:

Ightham Mote, Kent
The Vyne, Hampshire

The Three Feathers
The symbol of the Princes of Wales

Pomegranate, quiver of arrows and castle

Symbols of the Spanish princess Catherine of Aragon, Henry VIII's first wife.

The Tudor colours were green and white.

Why not think of a symbol for your own family?

HENRY VII
KEEPING THE PEACE 1485-1509

Henry VII did his best to unite the houses of York and Lancaster by marrying Elizabeth of York in 1486. However, other members of Edward IV's family and supporters refused to give up their claim and Henry's reign was dogged by rebellions.

The mysterious disappearance of Edward IV's sons – the Princes in the Tower – meant that Henry's enemies had a card up their sleeve. If they could persuade people to believe that they had found either of the princes, the true heirs to the throne, they might be able to overthrow Henry.

HENRY VII

Monkey business

Henry VII was understandably very distrustful of everyone. He was also very precise, keeping books full of notes on all sorts of subjects and insisting on checking accounts personally. His courtiers were worried about what he was writing in his journals and there is a story that one of them set the king's pet monkey loose in the same room where Henry's main book was kept. Much to the courtiers' delight the monkey ripped the book to shreds.

Takeover!

The first 'pretender' to the throne was Lambert Simnel who claimed to be the Earl of Warwick, Edward IV's nephew. Simnel and his supporters tried to overthrow Henry but they were defeated at the Battle of Stoke in 1487. Henry realised that Simnel – who was only ten – could not have been the brains behind the plan but had just been used as a pawn and so put him to work in the royal kitchens. He later became trainer of the king's hawks.

Just a few years later the Yorkists tried again. This time a young man named Perkin Warbeck was chosen to pretend to be Richard, the younger of the Princes in the Tower. But Perkin and his supporters were also beaten by Henry's army in 1491 and Perkin escaped to Ireland and then to Scotland. In 1497 Perkin tried again – this time with the help of the Scottish king – but was caught and imprisoned in the Tower of London. He met the real Earl of Warwick in jail and together they plotted to escape and overthrow Henry VII. This time, when they were found out, Henry decided to put an end to Warbeck altogether and executed him along with Warwick.

Morton's fork

Henry's chief minister and Archbishop of Canterbury, John Morton, invented a scheme of loans which meant that the rich couldn't become too powerful and kept the nobles under Henry's thumb. People who made a great show of their wealth were forced to give money to the crown because Morton said they obviously could afford it. Meanwhile people who seemed to live a simpler life were also told to cough up because they must be saving lots of money. This 'no win', two-pronged argument became known as Morton's Fork.

Preventative measures

Henry was aware that his position as king was under constant threat so he passed laws banning people from owning private armies and building castles. This was to stop any of the nobles becoming powerful enough to challenge him from within England.

Mix and match

Henry was very keen to avoid war as he knew how expensive and damaging it was. He tried to arrange marriage matches to make sure England had allies and to assure peace. His daughter Margaret was married to James IV of Scotland. His other daughter, Mary, was engaged to the future Holy Roman Emperor, Charles V, but ended up marrying Louis XII of France. Maybe the most important match was that of his elder son and heir, Arthur, who was married to the Spanish princess, Catherine of Aragon, in 1501. Arthur died the following year and Henry lost no time in betrothing Catherine to his second son, Henry, to save the Anglo-Spanish alliance. The results of this marriage changed English history.

MORTON'S FORK IN ACTION

Europe

In the sixteenth century, Spain was the most powerful country in Europe. Charles V ruled over a Spanish Empire, which included the Low Countries (now Holland and Belgium), Burgundy and Southern Italy, so it wasn't surprising that Henry wanted to keep on the right side of Charles.

There are two reasons why Spain held so much power. Firstly, Charles V inherited Spanish lands from his mother, as well as other parts of Europe from his grandfather, who was also the Holy Roman Emperor. The other reason was that Spanish explorers started colonies in the Americas and took over the gold and silver mines belonging to Aztecs. They brought great wealth back to Europe, but this actually caused problems – the flood of money coming in to Europe created terrible inflation.

Explorers from all over Europe (notably Portugal, France, Holland and Spain, as well as England) were discovering new countries and better trading routes, returning from their adventures with fabulous treasures and strange new food (read more about these explorers on page 20).

HENRY VIII SUPERMAN 1509-47

Henry VIII, who came to the thone in 1509, is probably the most famous king in English history. He was a figure larger than life and it's difficult to forget anyone who had six wives! Henry was a complicated character – he had bags of talent as a young man, but by the last few years of his reign he had become a ruthless, gross figure who distrusted everyone. What is more he left England in a weak state with his son Edward, only a young boy, to take over as king.

Sportsman

He was one of the best archers in the kingdom and loved jousting and hunting. Even in the year of his death when he was hideously overweight he insisted on being winched onto his horse to go riding.

Musician

He loved music and, as well as being an accomplished dancer, could sing and play the lute (one of the first types of guitar) and the virginals (a keyboard instrument). Legend has it that he was the 'anon' who wrote and composed the well-known song 'Greensleeves'.

Linguist

He spoke French, English and Latin fluently and could get by in Italian.

You would have thought that a man like Henry would have been happy. Unfortunately not. What Henry wanted more than anything else was a son to take over from him when he died and this is where his problems started.

FOR BETTER OR FOR WORSE

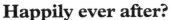

Although Henry VIII got through six wives he was actually married to his first wife, Catherine of Aragon, for nearly half his life. The rot set in when he divorced Catherine in 1533 and in ten years managed to say 'I do' to five different women ...

Happily ever after?

Henry came to the throne in April 1509 and less than two months later married his brother's widow, Catherine. Their first child was born dead the following year but in 1511 Henry organised a royal tournament to celebrate the birth of a prince. The baby died ten days later. Catherine must have had an awful time for in the next fifteen years – in spite of being pregnant several times – only one child, Mary, born in 1516, lived. Henry was desperate for a male heir and when Catherine was in her forties and past child-bearing Henry saw that the only way to get his heir was to divorce her. He had already chosen the woman to take over, Anne Boleyn, a lively, twenty-year-old whom he'd been courting for some time, and who he was certain would provide him with a healthy male heir.

Match the wives to their fate ...

Catherine of Aragon	*Beheaded*
Anne Boleyn	*Divorced*
Jane Seymour	*Bingo! outlives*
Anne of Cleves	*Died*
Catherine Howard	*Divorced*
Catherine Parr	*Beheaded*

Henry's solution

Nowadays divorce is very common – one in three marriages in England end in divorce, but in sixteenth-century England it hardly ever happened. Marriages were for life. The reason behind this was that the Church in England was controlled by the Pope in Rome, head of the Catholic Church, which was – and still is – very anti-divorce. Henry thought he would be able to divorce Catherine because he was a king and also knew that there was a passage in the Bible which said that a man should not marry his brother's widow, which is what he had done. Unfortunately for Henry, there were a few little problems which needed ironing out...

Permission granted

Henry's father, Henry VII, had got over the Biblical passage by getting special permission from the previous Pope for the marriage.

Relative values

Catherine was the aunt of Charles V, the Holy Roman Emperor. The current Pope, Clement, had been a prisoner of Charles and would have been in deep trouble if he agreed to Henry's demand to end the marriage.

OAK GALLERY, THE VYNE

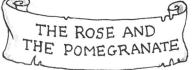

THE ROSE AND THE POMEGRANATE

Break up

Matters came to a head in 1532 when with the help of one of his chief advisers, Thomas Cromwell, Henry saw that the only way to get his marriage dissolved was to break away from the control of the Pope completely. Henry declared himself Head of the Church in England, married Anne and persuaded Archbishop Cranmer to declare his marriage to Catherine of Aragon at an end. Catherine was sent away from court and put in the charge of Sir Edmund Bedingfeld of Oxburgh Hall in Norfolk.

OXBURGH HALL

Tell-tale signs

When Henry married Catherine of Aragon in 1509 most people assumed that it would be for life. Loyal subjects decorated their houses with the Tudor rose and the pomegranate.

If you visit The Vyne in Hampshire you'll be able to see Henry's and Catherine of Aragon's symbols carved in the panelling of the Oak Gallery, showing the rose and pomegranate growing off the same stem to signify the bonding of the two families by marriage. Stained-glass windows in the chapel show Henry and Catherine happily married. Lord Sandys, the loyal subject who'd ordered all this decoration, must have had a few worries when Henry VIII came to visit with Anne Boleyn in 1535. No one knows if he tried to hide the evidence to avoid embarrassing the King and his new Queen.

There are more symbols from The Vyne in the Tudor Puzzle on page 10.

Martin Luther and the Reformation

Although most of Europe was Catholic before Henry made the break with Rome, many people were not happy that the Pope was head of the Church. Martin Luther was a German priest who criticised the Pope and various aspects of Catholic ceremony and belief. He wanted major reforms so this movement was known as the Reformation. Luther had many followers throughout Europe who became known as Protestants.

Tactless

When Catherine of Aragon died in 1536, Henry and Anne celebrated with an enormous banquet and jousting match and both wore bright yellow clothes 'in mourning'.

A new start

Anne had given birth to a baby girl in September 1533, Princess Elizabeth, but although Anne had another baby, it didn't survive. Less than three years after their marriage Henry accused Anne of being unfaithful and had her executed.

Take three ....

Wife number three was Jane Seymour who, in October 1537, gave birth to the boy, Edward, Henry had been waiting for. The price was high – she died twelve days later.

The camera never lies ...

Henry's next marriage was a disaster but at least the Queen escaped with her life. It may seem odd to us now, but marriages were often settled without the couple ever having met. Henry had been shown a portrait of Anne of Cleves, a Protestant princess from Germany, and agreed to marry her. He had a nasty shock when she arrived in England as she looked nothing like her portrait. The marriage went ahead in 1540 but they never lived together and Henry divorced her a few months later which, of course, was no problem now that he was Head of the Church. He was so angry with his chief minister, Thomas Cromwell, for suggesting the marriage that he had him executed.

Five gold rings

Henry turned back to home for the choice of his next wife so that there could be no cases of mistaken identity. He picked out a pretty seventeen-year-old, Catherine Howard, and they were married a month after his divorce from Anne of Cleves. Unfortunately she was TOO pretty! Henry was convinced she was being unfaithful and had her executed after little more than a year.

Last but not least

Catherine Parr was Henry's last wife. She had had some experience in the marriage game, having been widowed twice before, and proved to be a good companion to Henry in his last years. She managed to survive accusations of unfaithfulness and unsound religious beliefs and outlived Henry. She married for the fourth time a few months after Henry's death in 1547, but the following year she suffered the same fate as Jane Seymour, dying in childbirth.

The end result

Six wives later Henry had three surviving children: Mary, Elizabeth and Edward. All three of them were to reign England and none had any children.

Who's Who Game

Match these symbols from the Oak Gallery in The Vyne to the famous Tudor names below. Sir Reginald Bray's symbol is bray hemp (a bray is a crusher used for crushing plants such as hemp), but can you work out the others?

A

B

C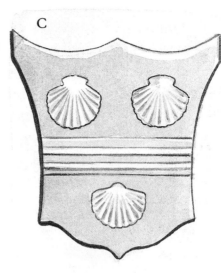

D

E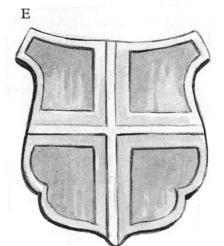

F

1. Thomas Wolsey   **2.** Richard Fox   **3.** Catherine of Aragon

4. St George   **5.** Shelley   **6.** Lord Sandys

If you want to know what some of the well-known Tudor characters looked like, visit Montacute in Somerset, and see the portraits hanging in the Long Gallery.

THE DISSOLUTION OF THE MONASTERIES

THOMAS CROMWELL

Once Henry had declared himself Head of the English Church he instantly became owner of all the monasteries, priories and nunneries and other Church property throughout the country. This was almost a quarter of all the land in England and Wales. Thomas Cromwell came up with the idea of closing these religious houses and selling off the property.

Most of Henry's reasons for getting rid of the monasteries came down to MONEY. The Crown was greatly in need of funds and by taking over monastic land, Henry could sell it off and pocket the cash. A reason was needed for such drastic action, so Henry sent commissioners to all the monasteries: they reported that in some, monks and nuns were enjoying too much luxury, while others were half empty and falling apart.

In all, 800 religious houses were swept away and 9,000 monks, nuns and friars found themselves without anywhere to live. What had even more effect was the loss of work for ordinary people who ran the monastic farms and industries.

FOUNTAINS ABBEY

Abbey conversions

Cromwell's scheme is why many of the monasteries, like Buckland Abbey in Devon, came to be converted into private houses. Some were demolished by their new owners to use the stone to build new houses. Others, like Fountains Abbey, in Yorkshire were in such isolated places that they were unsuitable as homes, and went into decay. Hundreds of years later some of the abbeys which had become picturesque ruins were used as features of landscape gardens.

National Trust properties to visit which used to be monasteries or religious houses:

Lacock Abbey, Wiltshire
Mount Grace Priory, North Yorkshire
Fountains Abbey, North Yorkshire
Buckland Abbey, Devon
Rievaulx Abbey (English Heritage), North Yorkshire

Two Young Monarchs Edward VI and Lady Jane

How would you feel if you were crowned King of England before you were old enough to leave primary school? Henry's son and heir, Edward, was only nine years old when he was crowned in 1547. His future did not look too rosy. Quite apart from the fact that he had little power himself and was being used as a puppet by powerful noblemen, he was clearly not a strong child: he was pale, thin and small for his age. In Tudor England, long before the discovery of today's range of medicines, only the strongest survived and although Edward lived through an attack of measles and smallpox in 1552 his body was weakened and he died of tuberculosis in July 1553.

EDWARD VI

Treason!

Edward's chief adviser was his uncle Edward Seymour, now Duke of Somerset. Seymour was so unpopular that even his younger brother, Lord Thomas Seymour, plotted against him. In 1549, with William Sharington (the new owner of Lacock Abbey in Wiltshire), he was arrested and accused of trying to overthrow the King. Sharington was the second-in-command at the Bristol Mint and had been providing Thomas with money to finance the plot. He confessed, blaming his partner-in-crime for everything, and Thomas was executed but Sharington got away with just a heavy fine.

EDWARD BEING USED AS A PUPPET

Church changes

In his five years as king, Edward and his advisers, or Council, who helped him rule, left their mark on England. He was an intelligent and very religious child and was determined to encourage the Protestant faith, as opposed to the Catholic Church from which his father had split. Edward's Council introduced laws that meant priests had to give services in English, not Latin, and wear plain clothes, and their churches had to be simply decorated. As a result thousands of paintings on church walls were whitewashed over, stained glass was smashed, and statues, carvings and pictures were taken away and often destroyed. Books from religious libraries were given away and there were even stories of shop owners using pages from valuable medieval illuminated (decorated) manuscripts as wrapping paper!

LACOCK ABBEY

Lady Jane

By 1552 it was obvious to Edward's advisers that the child was not going to live long. Edward wasn't married, let alone had any children, so people began to worry about who was going to take over when he died. Edward was desperate to keep England Protestant and knew that if his elder sister Mary became queen she would return the country to the Catholic faith. So, with the encouragement of his adviser, the Duke of Northumberland, he named as his heir the Protestant Lady Jane Grey, a great-granddaughter of Henry VII. It was no coincidence that Lady Jane was married to Northumberland's son, Guildford Dudley.

Lady Jane seems to have had a fairly miserable life. From her earliest days her mother and father used her as a pawn, planning that Jane should marry her cousin, King Edward. When Jane was nine she was sent to live in Catherine Parr's household at Chelsea, where she was probably happiest. Under Cathcrine's influence she became a devout Protestant.

The nine-day queen

Jane was highly educated and seems to have loved her studies, unlike her parents who had no interest in books and spent most of their time hunting. Her mother, in particular, was cruel to her and beat her often.

Things went horribly wrong for Jane when her scheming parents realised that Edward was not going to survive long and so quickly married her off to one of Northumberland's sons, Guildford Dudley. When Edward died, his Will said that Jane was to be queen before either of his two half-sisters. And so, at the age of fifteen, Jane was quickly crowned Queen of England.

A Tudor Wordsearch

L	U	M	S	D	A	Q	U	D	N
A	Y	R	E	S	I	T	O	O	F
G	R	N	L	L	K	C	M	M	A
S	E	W	T	F	A	M	E	I	R
F	O	O	T	B	A	L	L	N	C
B	J	C	I	G	E	I	Z	O	H
G	N	I	K	W	A	H	K	E	E
S	P	C	S	L	T	I	F	S	R
M	A	S	Q	U	E	T	X	L	Y
B	O	R	T	H	T	I	K	S	O

Find these nine Tudor games and pastimes

FOOTBALL
HAWKING
SKITTLES
DICE
BACKGAMMON
BOWLS
DOMINOES
ARCHERY
MASQUE (a play with music and dancing)

Answers on page 32

Mary's challenge

Meanwhile, Princess Mary escaped to East Anglia where she knew she had friends and raised an army to claim the throne. Northumberland had miscalculated badly and suddenly found himself with no supporters. He tried to do a U-turn and profess loyalty to Mary but was thrown into the Tower of London along with his son and daughter-in-law, where they were all eventually executed. Jane was queen for just nine days.

Bloody Mary 1553-58

Mary had the support of the country when she came to the throne but very soon managed to lose it. She was a very strong Catholic and wanted to make England a Catholic country again. In 1554 she married Philip II of Spain: she hoped to link the two Catholic countries and to provide an heir to the throne, even though she was thirty-seven when she married. This was not a popular move with English noblemen, who were worried about losing their lands that they'd got from Henry VIII's dissolution of the monasteries. What's more, Philip dragged England into war with France, a disaster that meant Calais was lost – England's last foothold in France. Mary never forgave herself and said that when she died they would find the word Calais written on her heart.

Wyatt's rebellion

In 1554, when it was learnt that Mary was planning to marry Philip of Spain, Sir Thomas Wyatt led a rebellion of Protestants from Kent, but was defeated by Mary's soldiers when they reached London. Wyatt was executed and hundreds of his supporters were hanged. This marked the beginning of the persecution of Protestants in England. During Mary's short reign many fled the country and more than 300 were burnt to death at the stake for heresy. This is how Mary got her nickname 'Bloody Mary'.

THOMAS WYATT

Counter measures

There were various anti-Catholic plots to put Mary's half-sister, Elizabeth, on the throne, so the Princess was put under close supervision. First, Elizabeth was kept in the Tower of London under the care of Sir Henry Bedingfeld, whose father had been custodian of Catherine of Aragon thirty years earlier. She was then moved to Woodstock near Oxford, again under Bedingfield's care. Sir Henry was a strict jailer but when Elizabeth became queen she showed no hard feelings and joked with him that if she ever needed to have someone well guarded, she knew whom to ask.

THE BELL TOWER, TOWER OF LONDON

ELIZABETH AGED 12

A bad start

Mary had had a sad childhood. When her father's marriage to Catherine of Aragon came to an end, she was declared illegitimate. Anne Boleyn hated her, stripped her of her title of princess and made her lady-in-waiting to Princess Elizabeth. Mary never saw her mother again although they did manage to write to each other in secret.

A fruitless reign

When Mary was dying in 1558 she must have known that all her hard work of trying to turn England back into a Catholic country would go to waste. Although twice she had convinced herself that she was pregnant, they were false alarms and she left her throne to Elizabeth, her Protestant half-sister.

ELIZABETH THE GREAT 1558-1603

Elizabeth I was probably the most shrewd of the Tudor monarchs. She chose loyal and skilled advisers like William Cecil and Sir Francis Walsingham. She took her duties as Queen extremely seriously and didn't let personal matters override as her father had done.

Queen's pet

Elizabeth had a series of favourite courtiers. They included the explorer and poet Sir Walter Raleigh, Robert Dudley, Earl of Leicester and, later, Leicester's stepson Robert Devereux, Earl of Essex. Although she seems to have loved Leicester deeply she ruled out marrying him because she knew it would split the kingdom and she put her duties as queen above all. She was so upset when he died in 1589 that she locked herself in her room and only came out when her door was broken down by worried staff. When she died fourteen years later, Leicester's last letter to her was found in a drawer by her bed.

THE EARL OF LEICESTER

THE EARL OF ESSEX

How the mighty are fallen

The Earl of Essex caught her eye but he misjudged how much power he enjoyed. Sent to Ireland in 1598 to fight the rebels who were against English rule, he did not follow Elizabeth's orders and failed in his mission. The Queen was furious. Essex fled back to London to explain, bursting in on Elizabeth before she'd got dressed, made-up or wigged – not a popular move. More blunders followed and Essex fell from favour, finally being executed for treason in 1601.

Unforgettable

Elizabeth was a striking looking woman, with auburn hair, white skin and pale eyes. Like her father and her half-sister and half-brother she was intelligent, very well educated and spoke English, Latin, French, Spanish, Italian, Flemish, Irish, Cornish and Welsh!

Number one

She was also very jealous and vain. Ladies at court had to dress in white and silver leaving the Queen to stand out in bright colours. In 1563 she gave an order that she had to approve all portraits of her and as she became older she ensured that they made her look young and beautiful. In 1596 she ordered that all 'unseemly' portraits of her be destroyed. There is a particularly ugly picture of Henry VIII in old age looking fat, bald and mean – perhaps Elizabeth wanted to stop anyone doing the same to her. When Elizabeth died she left over 3,000 dresses and head decorations.

Temper, temper ...

Elizabeth had a fierce temper: her godson, Sir John Harington, once said that he would rather face the entire Spanish army than the Queen in a rage.

COCKFIGHTING

Elizabethan entertainment

Elizabethans from all walks of life enjoyed games and sport as well as music, dancing and visiting the theatre. Today we would find some Elizabethan sport bloodthirsty or cruel. A popular pastime was watching a public execution, for example; another crowd-puller was cock fighting (the birds had metal spurs attached to their feet and had to scratch each other to death).

Travelling players visited villages, performing their plays in the open air, and the theatres in London were popular with both rich and poor. The poorer people, known as 'groundlings', sat on the ground around the edge of the stage and would sometimes throw things at the actors if they did not like the play.

MARY QUEEN OF SCOTS

When Elizabeth came to the throne she was prepared to try to keep both Protestants and Catholics happy in England for the sake of peace. She was a Protestant, but Catholics were given a fair amount of freedom and not persecuted in the way that they had been in Edward's reign or as the Protestants had suffered under Mary. Unfortunately this state of affairs was changed by the arrival in England of Mary Queen of Scots.

Who's the real queen?

Although Elizabeth I was Henry VIII's daughter, many Catholic subjects thought that she should not be queen because she was the child of Henry's second marriage which they had never accepted as legal. Instead, they supported the claim of Mary Queen of Scots, the Catholic granddaughter of Henry VIII's sister Margaret and James IV of Scotland.

Mary was a huge headache for Elizabeth. In 1567 Mary fled from Scotland where the Protestant lords had rebelled against her after she was involved in a number of scandals, and threw herself at the mercy of her English cousin. The last thing Elizabeth wanted was to have her main enemy to the throne on the spot but she saw no alternative and so kept her as her 'prisoner' in the north of England, away from court. Elizabeth and Mary never met.

Some of the Catholics in England viewed Mary as their leader and there were several plots to murder Elizabeth and put her on the throne. In 1580 the Pope even announced that it would not be a sin to kill Elizabeth. Most of Elizabeth's advisers were keen for Mary to be executed but Elizabeth was reluctant. Eventually they obtained evidence that Mary was directly involved in the Babington Plot and she was tried and found guilty of treason. It took Elizabeth three months to sign the death warrant and even then she had second thoughts. On 8 February 1587 Mary was executed in Fotheringhay in Northamptonshire and church bells rang in celebration for twenty-four hours in London. Elizabeth was furious, claiming that the execution had been a mistake and that she'd never agreed to it.

National Trust connections

The Throckmorton family of Coughton Court in Warwickshire were devout Catholics and supported Mary. Sir Nicholas Throckmorton, who had been Ambassador to Paris, was thrown into prison by Elizabeth for his friendship with Mary. His nephew was executed for his part in one of the plots to make Mary Queen of England.

Sir Thomas Sackville, 1st Earl of Dorset, who was given Knole in Kent by his cousin, Elizabeth I, sat at the trial of Anthony Babington, leader of the Babington Plot. It was this plot that spelt Mary's end, and it was Sackville who was given the job of telling her that she had been sentenced to death.

Sir Ralph Sadleir of Sutton House in Hackney had been Henry VIII's ambassador to Scotland, although he particularly loathed the Scots. Appropriately, he was one of the judges at Mary's trial. He wrote from Edinburgh, 'Under the sun live not more beastly and unreasonable people than be here'!

Lord Shrewsbury

Mary was put under the guardianship of Lord Shrewsbury from 1569 to 1584. Shrewsbury was married to Bess of Hardwick; they had a fiery relationship which ended in separation in 1584 after Bess claimed that Shrewsbury had been having an affair with the Scottish Queen. Mary was treated very well during her custody and had about fifty of her own servants but she was obviously bored. She was a skilled embroiderer and passed the hours sewing. You can see some of the pieces she made if you visit Hardwick Hall in Derbyshire or Oxburgh Hall in Norfolk. She used illustrations from a Herbal (book on plants) and Bestiary (book about animals) as ideas for her subjects.

To make a pattern, Mary would have used a pin to prick out the shape on the page of the book and then shaken soot onto the paper, holding it over the material to be embroidered. The soot would give the outline of the pattern.

Religious persecution

The Pope's declaration that it wasn't a sin to kill Elizabeth resulted in disaster for Catholics in England. Heavy fines were put on people who refused to give up their faith and many priests had to go into hiding. One of the best-known Catholic families of the day were the Ferrers from Baddesley Clinton in Warwickshire. The house became a hiding place for many priests on the run and had three different priest holes. The largest priest hole saved nine Catholics in October 1591 who hid in the drain up to their knees in water for four hours while troops searched the house.

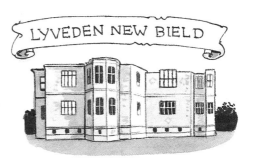

Concrete evidence

Other Catholics defied the ban in different ways. Sir Thomas Tresham chose a bad time to be converted to Catholicism but declared his faith by building a lodge called Lyveden New Bield in Northamptonshire, in the shape of a cross and with all sorts of messages in the stonework referring to the Catholic faith.

SEA DOGS

The Elizabethan Age was a time of discovery and exploration, with quests for new and quicker trade routes: European explorers discovered new lands and riches from the Far East were brought back to England. It was also an era of great buccaneering and piracy, with sailors like Francis Drake and Raleigh raiding Spanish ships returning from the wealthy American colonies, while Elizabeth turned a blind eye and took a slice of the profits.

COMPTON CASTLE

A family of sea dogs

Many of these daring Elizabethan seamen came from the West Country. Seafaring came naturally to the Gilbert family from Compton Castle in Devon. All three sons born in the mid-sixteenth century went to sea: John Gilbert was a vice Admiral and helped to defeat the Spanish Armada while his younger two brothers, Adrian and Humphrey, were both explorers. What's more, their half-brother was another famous sea dog, Sir Walter Raleigh.

Lost at sea

In 1583, Humphrey Gilbert claimed Newfoundland, on the east coast of America, for Elizabeth but on the return trip his ship, *The Squirrel,* sank with all hands and Gilbert was drowned. In the chapel at Compton Castle, squirrels have been carved on the pew ends in memory of this great explorer. Other efforts to set up colonies in North America by Raleigh and Richard Grenville, from Buckland Abbey in Devon, also failed.

A devilish captain

Francis Drake came from simple beginnings to be one of the most famous men in England. His life revolved around the sea. In his younger days he was involved in the slave trade with Africa but then concentrated on raiding Spanish treasure ships. His greatest voyage ended in 1580 when he returned to England in his ship, *The Golden Hind*, having sailed round the world and stolen a fortune from the Spanish colonies in South America. The Spanish hated Drake and believed that he had sold his soul to the devil to become such a brilliant sailor! He was to annoy the Spanish even more when he played a key part in the defeat of the Armada in 1588.

SIR FRANCIS DRAKE

BUCKLAND ABBEY

DRAKE'S DRUM

Drake was knighted by Elizabeth and bought a home for himself at Buckland Abbey in Devon. Buckland was once a monastery but it had been dissolved by Henry VIII and was then bought by the Grenville family. Sir Richard Grenville converted it into a country house but sold it pretty quickly to agents acting for Drake. If you visit you can see various objects belonging to Sir Francis including Drake's Drum. The legend goes that the drum will beat to call Drake back from the dead if ever England is in danger.

'Warter' Raleigh

Elizabeth used to call Walter Raleigh 'Warter', imitating his strong West Country accent. He was later given the more attractive nickname of 'Shepherd of the Ocean'. Raleigh spent a fortune impressing the Queen with his dress sense, including £6,000 (in modern money) on jewelled shoes!

SIR WALTER RALEIGH

THE ARMADA

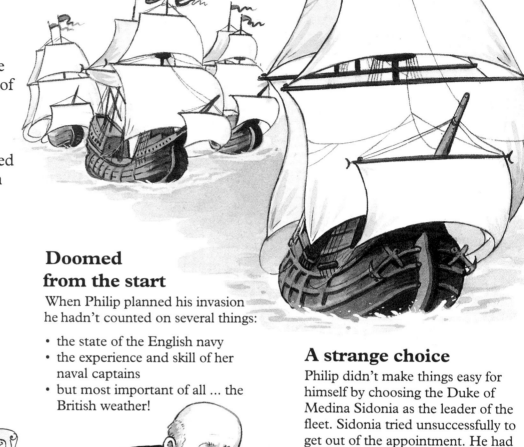

When Drake started attacking Spanish ships in their home ports, he infuriated Philip II of Spain so much that he was pushed to breaking point. Matters came to a head in 1587 when Elizabeth executed Mary Queen of Scots, whom Philip hoped would become the Catholic Queen of England, and he decided to invade England and make himself king. The result was one of the most famous English naval victories of all time – the defeat of the Spanish Armada.

PHILIP II OF SPAIN

Doomed from the start

When Philip planned his invasion he hadn't counted on several things:

- the state of the English navy
- the experience and skill of her naval captains
- but most important of all … the British weather!

A strange choice

Philip didn't make things easy for himself by choosing the Duke of Medina Sidonia as the leader of the fleet. Sidonia tried unsuccessfully to get out of the appointment. He had two very good reasons – apart from having no naval experience, he suffered horribly from seasickness.

THE DUKE OF MEDINA SIDONIA

A man's world

While the Armada was sailing up the English Channel, Elizabeth I gave a stirring speech to her troops at Tilbury, just east of London, when she said:

'I have but the body of a weak and feeble woman, but I have the heart and stomach of a king, and a king of England too and think foul scorn that any Prince in Europe should dare to invade the borders of my realm.'

The country was so united against the invasion that even English Catholics supported Elizabeth.

Shipwreck!

Philip's plan was for the Armada to pick up soldiers from the Spanish Netherlands and then invade England. The Armada never reached Holland. It sailed up the Channel, chased by English ships, and anchored at Calais where Drake sent in fire ships to break it up. With his fleet separated and damaged Sidonia realised that the battle was lost and concentrated on getting the navy back to Spain.

The Spanish had little choice in their route home – they had to try to sail all the way round Scotland and down the west coast of Ireland. The weather was terrible and many ships were wrecked off Scotland and Ireland. One ship, *The Girona*, came to its end off the Giant's Causeway in Northern Ireland – only five people from the 1, 300 men on board survived.

THE ROUTE OF THE ARMADA

A great loss

Over 80 Spanish ships were destroyed in the Armada campaign and 10,000 Spanish troops and sailors died.

Shining like a beacon

The English had a good network of hill-top beacons which were lit to alert troops and warn the population in times of danger. The beacons were lit in 1588 although the Spanish never actually landed on English soil. Armada beacon sites owned by the National Trust include Golden Cap in Dorset and Roseberry Topping in Yorkshire.

GOLDEN CAP HILL

A glorious reign

After the defeat of the Armada, Elizabeth became a legend in her own lifetime. She ruled England for another fifteen years and her death in 1603 marked the end of the Tudor dynasty. She named as her heir James Stuart, the son of Mary Queen of Scots.

HEALTH AND HYGIENE

People in Tudor England often had a bad diet which resulted in various vitamin deficiencies. Teeth decayed through eating too many sweet things and not cleaning them properly. Look at this recipe for tooth paste and you'll understand why ...

Honey

Sugar

Crushed bones

Fruit peel

Soot

Once their teeth became stained they tried to remove marks by rubbing them with powdered pumice stone, alabaster (similar to marble), crushed brick or coral. The process was finished by rinsing the mouth with wine or sugary water.

Gone to seed

In the last years of his life Henry VIII was a sorry sight. His body was showing distinct signs of wear and tear. From the symptoms described – leg ulcers, stomach pains, coughing and depression – it could have been that Henry was suffering from scurvy, a disease caused by lack of vitamin C from fresh fruit and vegetables (rich people in the sixteenth century thought these were more suitable for peasants to eat, so they stuck to a diet of meat, fish and sweet dishes). Henry had become so fat that he needed winches and pulleys to get him upstairs. His bed was four metres wide.

A right royal doctor

Robert Huickes was physician to Henry VIII, Edward VI and Elizabeth I. You can still see part of the house which he built for himself at Nunnington Hall in Yorkshire.

NUNNINGTON HALL

Let it out

Mary I suffered from depression and believed that if she was blooded (cut by a doctor to let the 'bad' blood out) she would be cured. The Venetian ambassador thought this could be the reason why she always looked pale and thin.

What a pong!

People did not wash frequently in Tudor times and often became pretty smelly. To disguise the stink people would carry pomanders – sometimes oranges studded with cloves – to wave a sweet scent around. Elizabeth I took more baths than most, but she only took the plunge once a month!

Flushed with success

Toilet facilities were very basic although Sir John Harington – Queen Elizabeth's godson – came up with an invention for a primitive type of flushing lavatory and advised her to install it in her palace at Richmond. Harington was a bit of a practical joker, so he wasn't taken seriously.

Crowning glory

Women who wanted blonde hair dyed it with rhubarb and white wine. Fair hair was in great demand and often women would pay children for their hair to make wigs. Frizzy hair was the fashion and styles were decorated with jewels and gold. Wigs were also common – Mary Queen of Scots and Elizabeth I both wore them.

If looks could kill

The pursuit of the perfect skin could be very dangerous. Pale complexions were fashionable and women used a mixture of white lead and vinegar to whiten their skin. This not only whitened but withered the skin and could paralyse. To make matters worse the preferred blusher was mercuric sulphide, a chemical which eventually ate away the skin.

Uncomfortable fashion

During Tudor times the dress hoop, or farthingale, was worn by most noble women. This was a wire cage shaped like a drum and fastened around the waist which made the skirt stick out on either side for half a metre and then drop straight down to the floor. It must have been pretty difficult to sit down ...

Stiff as a board

Another major introduction was starch which was brought over from France in the 1590s. It was known as the 'devil's liquor' and meant that people could wear huge ruffs without them flopping. Things got a little out of hand and men in particular wore enormous plate-like constructions around their necks thanks to the wonders of starch!

Jewels galore!

Clothing worn by the aristocracy tended to be highly ornate and there was a certain amount of recycling of decoration when the fabric became worn. In 1517 450 ounces of gold and 850 pearls were removed from old clothes of Henry VIII to be re-used. If you look closely at the appliquéed hangings in the Entrance Hall at Hardwick, you'll see that the velvets and silks from medieval church vestments (robes) have been cut up and included in the design.

An Englishman's Home is His Castle

Until the beginning of the sixteenth century, country houses had been built to resist attack. This meant that they often were like mini castles, with moats, arrow slits for windows and would look onto a courtyard rather than have a garden. But by the end of the century, people began to feel more confident. The Spanish had failed to invade, the wool trade was prospering, people were better educated, and many had travelled and seen styles of architecture in Europe which they felt like copying on their return to England.

Bess the builder

Hardwick Hall in Derbyshire must have cost Elizabeth Shrewsbury (Bess of Hardwick) a fortune to build as it has huge areas of windows. Of course, this meant that in winter it was absolutely freezing and in summer it was too hot. However, Bess could easily afford it – she was the second richest woman in England (after the queen) and had extravagant tastes. Her bedcover was made of black velvet embroidered with silver and pearls and when she died in 1608 over £1,500 was spent on cloth for the funeral – that is over £30,000 in today's money.

Expensive tastes

Glass was very expensive in Tudor England. People used to take windows with them when they moved house until 1579 when a law was passed banning it. The more windows a house had, the richer the owner was. William Moreton added new windows to his house, Little Moreton Hall in Cheshire, as a symbol of his wealth.

LITTLE MORETON HALL

Home comforts

Houses were becoming a lot more comfortable and pleasant to live in than they had been in the Middle Ages. As windows replaced arrow slits there was more natural light, and proper chimneys were built so rooms were less smoky. Floors were still covered with rushes but they tended to be woven together as mats rather than just lying loose.

BESS OF HARDWICK

Fancy a walk?

Another feature of Tudor stately homes was the long gallery. This was a long, narrow room which was well lit and often stretched from one end of the house to the other, such as the 60-metre long gallery at Montacute in Somerset. It was used for displaying treasures and paintings, and playing games and music, but mainly was designed as an exercise room when the weather was too bad outside. Some people used these rooms for playing sport: a tennis ball dating from Elizabethan times was found behind the panelling of the long gallery at Little Moreton Hall. You can see other long galleries at Blickling Hall in Norfolk, The Vyne in Hampshire, Hardwick Hall in Derbyshire, Lanhydrock in Cornwall and Ightham Mote in Kent (now a chapel).

LONG GALLERY

HARDWICK HALL

LONG GALLERY

LITTLE MORETON HALL

I'd LOVE you to come but …

Some people who couldn't face the hassle and expense of a royal visit tried, usually unsuccessfully, to put Elizabeth off visiting. In 1573 when she suggested coming to stay with the Archbishop of Canterbury he wrote back saying that there was an epidemic of plague, smallpox and measles in the area. It didn't work and Elizabeth's visit went ahead.

HOPING TO PUT OFF A VISIT BY ELIZABETH

Royal freebies

It was the practice of the Tudor court to go on royal 'progresses'. This meant that in the summer Queen Elizabeth with about 150 servants and courtiers would travel round the country staying with loyal subjects. There were several reasons for this:

- it meant that there was a chance to clean and de-stink the palaces in London
- Elizabeth didn't have to pay
- If one of her subjects was getting too powerful all the queen had to do was visit and stay for a long time. This meant that the expense of looking after her and the court would bankrupt the host!

Just in case

Many people built enormous grand houses in preparation for a royal visit – but sometimes the Queen never came. Hardwick Hall in Derbyshire, with its grand state rooms on the top floor, was built for a royal visit which never happened. Christopher Hatton, the royal treasurer, spent a fortune on building a huge house at Holdenby in Northamptonshire but again Elizabeth never visited it and it was demolished only eighty years later.

GARDEN PAVILION, MONTACUTE

Banquets

A banquet in Elizabethan times was not a huge meal but was more like the pudding or dessert course of a main meal. After the meat courses people would retire to another room to eat their dessert while the main room was cleared for dancing. These smaller rooms were known as banqueting houses and were very fashionable during Elizabethan times. Some were even built away from the house and used for separate dessert parties rather than part of the main evening celebrations. There's a garden pavilion at Montacute, for example, built for this very purpose.

FOOD AND FUN

The favourite sport of the aristocracy was hunting. Everyone could hunt hare but only gentlemen were allowed to chase deer, and manor houses used to be surrounded by deer parks. This meant that poaching was quite common. At Charlecote Park in Warwickshire the young playwright William Shakespeare was caught poaching deer and punished by the owner, Sir Thomas Lucy. Shakespeare got his own back by basing a comic character called Justice Shallow on Sir Thomas.

A wild country

Although animals like wolves, lynx, bears and elks had almost died out in Britain by the start of the Tudor era, there were still boars, wild cats and wild cattle roaming the forests.

Reduced horsepower

The horses people rode for hunting would have been much slower than the animals people ride today. This is because the much faster Arab horses had not yet been introduced to England and bred into local stock. The English horses were strong animals bred for carrying knights wearing armour.

SHAKESPEARE IS CAUGHT POACHING

HENRY VIII JOUSTING

Tournaments

Jousting was another popular horseback sport, although it could be highly dangerous. King Henry II of France was killed at a jousting tournament in 1559 when a lance splintered and pierced his chest, while Henry VIII had a close shave in 1536 when jousting with his visor open.

Anyone for tennis?

The game in which Henry VIII excelled was not lawn tennis, a nineteenth-century invention, but real (royal) tennis. This started as a game played against a castle wall in medieval France, which explains the odd shape of the court and the complex scoring. There are several real tennis courts in Britain, including one you can visit at Henry VIII's palace at Hampton Court.

Food, glorious food!

Eating in Tudor England was an important affair. The royal court in particular used to get through an enormous quantity of food – three-quarters of which was meat. A record at Hampton Court shows that in a single year of Henry VIII's reign the kitchens dealt with

1,240 oxen

8,200 sheep

2,300 deer

760 calves

1,870 pigs

53 wild boar

... and that didn't even include all the fish and poultry they ate! Tudors consumed some pretty strange things by our standards. The court menu would have featured larks, swans, peacocks, sparrows and even whale.

Heavily flavoured

Before the days of freezers and tinning factories the only way of keeping food from going rotten was to salt or sugar it heavily. People ate twice as much salt in their diet as today. Spices and herbs would be added to try to disguise the salty taste of meat and fish. Cloves, ginger and nutmeg would have come from the other side of the world from the Spice Islands in what is now Indonesia.

A LIGHT SNACK FOR HENRY VIII

Pigeon pie

Before winter feeding crops were grown, many animals were killed when the cold weather set in and the meat was preserved by salting. The sole supply of all-year-round fresh meat was from the pigeons kept in the dovecote, which made a pleasant change from salted beef. Only Lords of the Manor were allowed to build these birdhouses and you can see an unusual one built by Sir John Gostwick, a senior servant to Cardinal Wolsey, at Willington in Bedfordshire. Gostwick must have liked the taste of pigeon – his dovecote has 1,500 nesting boxes!

DOVECOTE WILLINGTON

SIR WALTER INTRODUCES THE POTATO TO ENGLAND

WALTER

Chips with everything?

It's difficult to believe now, but no-one had seen a potato in England before the end of the sixteenth century when Sir Walter Raleigh appeared with this strange new plant from his trip to North America. Even then, people considered it a decorative plant and it was many years before it became a common part of the English diet. Before then, people ate bread as an equivalent and stews – known as pottage – were thickened with barley and oats.

Have ye nyce daye

Implements

During the Tudor period, wooden plates and spoons were gradually replaced with plates made out of pewter and knives and spoons made out of tin or sometimes silver. No china or glass were used at the table.

TUDOR CHILDREN

In Tudor times babies from rich families would often have 'wet nurses'. These were women from poorer families who were paid to breastfeed babies – their own baby might have died or they might have been feeding two babies at once.

A tight start

Babies were swaddled at birth. This meant they were tightly wrapped from neck to toe in a long band of material about three metres long. This was supposed to make their legs and arms grow straight and children spent the first few months of their life in this uncomfortable wrapping. Babies had a pretty rough time of it and were sometimes hung up in their swaddling bands from a hook on the wall! Toddlers were protected from hurting their heads when they fell over by wearing a padded head band known as a 'pudding band' because it looked like a black pudding.

Coral charms

When babies were baptised, salt was put on the tongue and oil on the forehead. Children often wore a piece of coral which was supposed to be good luck and keep away evil and illness. If you look at paintings of children from this time, try to find this good luck charm.

A good training

Children of wealthy families were often sent to live with families from a still higher class for a couple of years. This was called 'placing out'. They would have household jobs to do but it was hoped that they would pick up some tips on manners and behaviour. Lady Jane Grey went to Catherine Parr's household and Bess of Hardwick met her first husband when they were both living at the Zouche family house in London.

NATIONAL TRUST HOUSES TO VISIT

MOSELEY OLD HALL

Baddesley Clinton, Warwickshire
Barrington Court, Somerset
Benthall Hall, Shropshire
Buckland Abbey, Devon
Charlecote Park, Warwickshire
Cotehele House, Cornwall
Coughton Court, Warwickshire
Fountains Abbey, Yorkshire
Hardwick Hall, Derbyshire
Ightham Mote, Kent
Knole, Kent
Lacock Abbey, Wiltshire
Little Moreton Hall, Cheshire
Lyveden New Bield, Northamptonshire
Melford Hall, Suffolk
Montacute, Somerset
Moseley Old Hall, Staffordshire
Mottisfont Abbey, Hampshire
Nunnington Hall, North Yorkshire
Oxburgh Hall, Norfolk
Paycocke's, Essex
Speke Hall, Merseyside
Sutton House, London
Trerice, Cornwall
Tudor Merchant's House, Dyfed
Ty Mawr, Gwynedd
The Vyne, Hampshire

ANSWERS

p.13 Tudor Wordsearch

```
L U M S D A Q U D N
A Y R E S I T O O F
G R N L L K C M M A
S E W T F A M E I R
F O O T B A L L N C
B J C I G E I Z O H
G N I K W A H K E E
S P C S L T I F S R
M A S Q U E T X L Y
B O R T H T I K S O
```

p.7 Match the wives

Catherine of Aragon – Divorced
Anne Boleyn – Beheaded
Jane Seymour – Died
Anne of Cleves – Divorced
Catherine Howard – Beheaded
Catherine Parr – Bingo! outlives Henry

p.10 Who's Who Game

A. 2   B. 6   C. 5
D. 3   E. 4   F. 1

First published in 1993 by National Trust (Enterprises) Ltd,
36 Queen Anne's Gate, London SW1H 9AS
Registered Charity No. 205846

Copyright © The National Trust 1993

ISBN   0 7078 0168 0

Designed by Blade Communications, Leamington Spa
Printed in England

IGHTHAM MOTE